Guide

TENNESSEE

By Carole Marsh

The GALLOPADE GANG

Carole Marsh	Kathy Zimmer	Cranston Davenport
Bob Longmeyer	Terry Briggs	Lisa Stanley
Chad Beard	Pat Newman	Antoinette Miller
Cecil Anderson	Billie Walburn	Victoria DeJoy
Steven Saint-Laurent	Jackie Clayton	Al Fortunatti
Jill Sanders	Pam Dufresne	Shery Kearney

Published by GALLOPADE INTERNATIONAL

www.tennesseeexperience.com
800-536-2GET • www.gallopade.com

©2004 Carole Marsh • Second Edition • All Rights Reserved.
Character Illustrations by Lucyna A. M. Green.
No part of this publication may be reproduced in whole or in part, stored in a retrieval system, or transmitted in any form or by any means, electronic, mechanical, photocopying, recording or otherwise, without written permission from the publisher.

The Tennessee Experience logo is a trademark of Carole Marsh and Gallopade International, Inc. A free catalog of The Tennessee Experience Products is available by calling 800-536-2GET, or by visiting our website at www.tennesseeexperience.com.

Gallopade is proud to be a member of these educational organizations and associations:

Other Tennessee Experience Products

- The Tennessee Experience!
- The BIG Tennessee Reproducible Activity Book
- The Tennessee Coloring Book
- My First Book About Tennessee!
- Tennessee "Jography": A Fun Run Through Our State
- Tennessee Jeopardy!: Answers and Questions About Our State
- The Tennessee Experience! Sticker Pack
- The Tennessee Experience! Poster/Map
- Discover Tennessee CD-ROM
- Tennessee "Geo" Bingo Game
- Tennessee "Histo" Bingo Game

A Word From the Author... (okay, a few words)...

Hi!

Here's your own handy pocket guide about the great state of Tennessee! It really will fit in a pocket—I tested it. And it really will be useful when you want to know a fact you forgot, to bone up for a test, or when your teacher says, "I wonder . . ." and you have the answer—instantly! Wow, I'm impressed!

Get smart, have fun!
Carole Marsh

Tennessee Basics explores your state's symbols and their special meanings!

Tennessee Geography digs up the what's where in your state!

Tennessee History is like traveling through time to some of your state's great moments!

Tennessee People introduces you to famous personalities and your next-door neighbors!

Tennessee Places shows you where you might enjoy your next family vacation!

Tennessee Nature - no preservatives here, just what Mother Nature gave to Tennessee!

All the real fun stuff that we just HAD to save for its own section!

- Tennessee Basics
- Tennessee Geography
- Tennessee History
- Tennessee People
- Tennessee Places
- Tennessee Nature
- Tennessee Miscellany

State Name

Who Named You?

Tennessee's official state name is...

Tennessee

State Name

Word Definition

OFFICIAL: appointed, authorized, or approved by a government or organization

Statehood: June 1, 1796

Tennessee was the 16th state to join the Union.

Tennessee will be on a state-commemorative quarter starting in the year 2002. Look for it in cash registers everywhere!

Coccinella noemnotata is my name (that's Latin for ladybug)! What's YOURS?

State Name Origin

What's In A Name?

State Name Origin

Tennessee got its name from a Native American word from the Yuchi language, *Tana-see* which means "The Meeting Place." Travelers in the 1700s associated the name with a Cherokee village and a river in Cherokee territory.

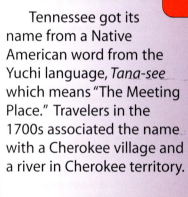

Many of Tennessee's city names, such as Chattanooga and Oneida, reflect its Native American heritage.

State Nicknames

WHO Are You Calling Names?

State Nicknames

Tennessee is not the only name by which the state is recognized. Like many other states, Tennessee has some nicknames, official or unofficial.

The Volunteer State

The Mother of Southwestern Statesmen

Big Bend State

Tennessee became known as The Volunteer State when thousands of Tennessee soldiers volunteered and fought bravely in the War of 1812.

State Capital/Capitol

State Capital: Nashville

State Capital/Capitol

Nashville was settled in 1780, incorporated in 1784, became capital of Tennessee in 1843.

Nashville is the "Country Music Capital of the World." It's also known as the "Athens of the South" and "Music City, USA."

Word Definition

CAPITAL: a town or city that is the official seat of government
CAPITOL: the building in which the government officials meet

State Government

Who's in Charge Here?

Tennessee's GOVERNMENT has three branches:

- **EXECUTIVE**
- **LEGISLATIVE**
- **JUDICIAL**

State Government

- **Executive:** A governor and department commissioners
- **Legislative:** Two Houses: Senate (33 members) House of Representatives (99 members)
- **Judicial:** Supreme Court: Chief Justice and four Associate Justices intermediate appellate, general trial courts, and courts of limited jurisdiction

The number of legislators is determined by population, which is counted every ten years; the numbers above are certain to change as Tennessee grows and prospers!

When you are 18 and register according to Tennessee laws, you can vote! So please do! Your vote counts!

State Flag

State Flag

Tennessee's current state flag was adopted in 1905. It features a geometric design of three white stars in a blue circle on a field of red. The stars represent three distinctly different regions, the Grand Divisions of the state—East, Middle, and West. The stars are eternally bound by an unending white band.

As you travel throughout Tennessee, count the times you see the Tennessee flag! Look for it on government vehicles, too!

State Seal & Motto

State Seal

The state of Tennessee features the state motto (Agriculture and Commerce), and pictures of a plow, a boat, wheat, and cotton. The Roman numeral XVI stands for Tennessee being the 16th state, and 1796 is the date of the state constitution.

MOTTO: a sentence, phrase, or word expressing the spirit or purpose of an organization or group

State Motto

Tennessee's state motto is... *"Agriculture and Commerce."*

Even before statehood, politicians tried to establish official seals. Records indicate that as early as 1772, the Articles of the Watauga Association authorized the use of a seal.

State Slogan

Tennessee's state slogan is...

"Tennessee— America at its Best"

State Bird

Birds of a Feather

The state bird of Tennessee is the mockingbird, *Mimus polyglottos*, known for its singing ability. It can also mimic other birds and even a dog's bark.

State Bird

Mockingbirds are known for their defensive behavior of the family nest. They've even been known to chase off crows and cats!

Tennessee has a state game bird, too! It's the bobwhite quail.

State Tree

Tulip Poplar
—*Liriodendron tulipifera*—

State Tree

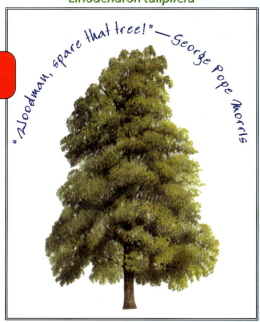

"Woodman, spare that tree!" —George Pope Morris

Tennessee's state tree is the tulip poplar. A relative of the magnolia family, the tulip poplar can live for years and years—200 in fact! It can sometimes grow to be 200 feet (61 meters) tall! The tulip poplar was named Tennessee's state tree because of its use by pioneers to build homes, barns, and other buildings.

State Flower

—Iridaceae—

State Flower

The iris was chosen by the state legislature in 1933 to be Tennessee's cultivated flower. Irises bloom in many different colors, but when people think of Tennessee's state flower, the color purple comes to mind.

A lovelier flower on earth was never sown.
— William Wordsworth

Tennessee also has a state wildflower. The passion flower's name comes from early Christian missionaries who saw an image of the crucifixion of Jesus Christ in the flower's parts.

RIDDLE:
If the state wildflower got mixed up with a firefly, one of the state insects, what would you have?

ANSWER: A passion flower that blinks—it could happen!

State Wild Animal

Raccoon
—*Procyon lotor*—

State Wild Animal

Raccoons often live in dens in hollow trees. Three to six babies are born in spring. The babies stay in the den for about two months and don't leave home for about a year.

Raccoons are furry mammals with bushy, ringed tails and black masks on their faces. Raccoons feed on fish and frogs they catch in rivers and streams. They also eat wild fruit and corn. Raccoons are neat and tidy; they wash their food when they're near water.

State Horse

TENNESSEE WALKING HORSE

The Tennessee Walking Horse is bred near Nashville. Tennessee Walkers have a long, graceful gait (stride) that's unique to this breed of saddle horse. They are bred to comfortably carry their riders for a long period of time. Tennessee Walkers also have a gentle disposition.

Tennessee Walking Horse became a recognized breed in 1935. Famous Tennessee Walkers include F Allen One and Strolling Jim.

For ten days each summer, folks get together in Shelbyville for "the Celebration." It's a famous festival and competition that's officially called the Tennessee Walking Horse National Celebration.

State Dance

The Square Dance

State Dance

The square dance is an American folk dance related to the English country dance and French ballroom dance. It includes squares, rounds, clogging, contra, line, the Virginia reel, and heritage dances.

The Virginia Reel is an American country dance in which the partners face each other in two lines and perform various steps to the instructions of a caller.

State Songs

Tennessee has many official state songs:

"My Homeland Tennessee" adopted in 1925
words by Nell Grayson Taylor
music by Roy Lamont Smith

"When It's Iris Time in Tennessee" adopted in 1935
by Willa Waid Newman

State Songs

"Tennessee Waltz" adopted in 1965
by Redd Stewart and Pee Wee King

"Rocky Top" adopted in 1982
by Boudleaux and Felice Bryant

"Tennessee" adopted in 1992
by Vivian Rorie

"The Pride of Tennessee" adopted in 1996
by Fred Congdon, Thomas Vaughn, and Carol Elliot

"My Tennessee" official public school song, adopted in 1955
by Francis Hannah Tranum

Tennessee has some special bicentennial songs, too: "The Tennessee Salute," "Fly Eagle, Fly," and "My Home Will Always Be In Tennessee." These songs commemorated the state's 200th birthday in 1996!

State Gem, Rock, and Stone

State Gem

Tennessee river pearls are found in mussels that live in freshwater rivers and come in different shapes, sizes, and colors. These pearls are completely made by the mussel, unlike cultured pearls which are partly man-made.

Tennessee river pearls are beautiful and durable. They're used to make rings, cuff links, and stick pins.

State Rock

In 1979, limestone was declared an official state rock. Limestone is found throughout Tennessee.

State Stone

Tennessee marble is a metamorphic (transformed) version of limestone. Marble is used throughout the country to make monuments and buildings.

Agate was designated the official state stone in 1969. It's a semiprecious gemstone found in only a few areas of the state.

State Insects

State Insects

Firefly (Photinus pyrallsis)
Ladybug (Coccinella noemnotata)

Tennessee has two state insects, the firefly and ladybug. Fireflies have a special light that shines white, yellow, orange, greenish blue, or red. In some types of fireflies, the females remain in the larvae stage and are called glowworms.

Ladybugs help Tennessee farmers by feeding on bugs that eat crops. In folk medicine, ladybugs were used as a cure for some types of diseases such as colic and measles.

State Insects

State Agricultural Insect

Honeybee (Apis mallifera)

Honeybees are important to Tennessee's economy. They pollinate many different crops, grasses, and trees. Honeybees also produce sweet-tasting honey and beeswax.

State Butterfly

Zebra Swallowtail
(Eurytides marcellus)

The zebra swallowtail butterfly was designated by the General Assembly in 1995 as Tennessee's official state butterfly. It has black and yellow stripes with red and blue spots and can be found throughout Tennessee.

State Fish

Sport Fish
Largemouth Bass (*Micropterus salmoides*)

State Fish

Tennessee's state sport fish, the largemouth bass, lives in freshwater lakes, ponds, and streams throughout the state. They prefer slow-moving waters that contain logs and debris. Largemouth bass are a favored fish of finicky fishermen!

Commercial Fish
Channel Catfish (*Ictalurus lacustris*)

Tennessee's state commercial fish is the channel catfish. Sometimes known as the "spotted cat" or "fiddler," the channel catfish is raised in farm ponds and may be found in many lakes and streams.

Tennessee Bass
Put a bass filet on foil. Drizzle with lemon juice. Sprinkle with salt and pepper. Add shredded smoked ham and broil fish until done.

Sounds fishy to me!

State Location

Tennessee is one of the southern states.

State Location

THE CONTIGUOUS UNITED STATES

Tennessee →

Word Definition

LATITUDE: Imaginary lines which run horizontally east and west around the globe
LONGITUDE: Imaginary lines which run vertically north and south around the globe

State Neighbors

These border Tennessee:

States: North Carolina, Virginia, Kentucky, Missouri, Arkansas, Mississippi, Alabama, Georgia

Body of Water: Mississippi River

State Neighbors

East-West, North-South, Area

I'll Take the Low Road...

Tennessee stretches 120 miles (193 kilometers) from north to south—or south to north. Either way, it's a long drive!

Total Area: Approximately 42,145 square miles (109,147 square kilometers)
Land Area: Approximately 41,219 square miles (106,749 square kilometers)

Tennessee is 491 miles (790 kilometers) from east to west—or west to east. Either way, it's *still* a long drive!

This is a compass rose. It helps you find the right direction on a map!

Highest & Lowest Points

You Take the High Road!

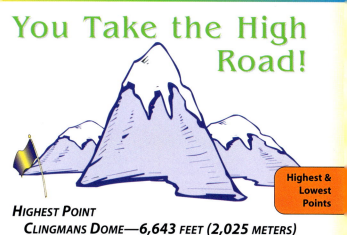

HIGHEST POINT
CLINGMANS DOME—6,643 FEET (2,025 METERS)

There are more than 16 peaks in the Smoky Mountains that are taller than 6,000 feet (1,829 meters).

LOWEST POINT
MISSISSIPPI RIVER—178 FEET (54 METERS)

State Counties

I'm County-ing on You!

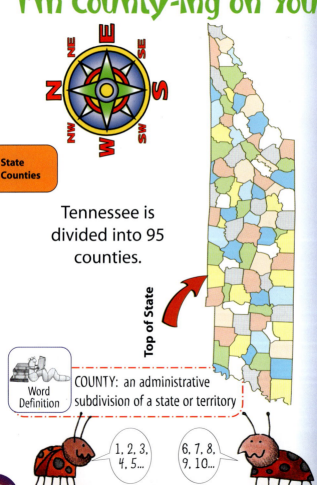

State Counties

Tennessee is divided into 95 counties.

Top of State

COUNTY: an administrative subdivision of a state or territory

Word Definition

1, 2, 3, 4, 5... 6, 7, 8, 9, 10...

Natural Resources

It's All Natural!

Forests cover about half the land area of Tennessee.

NATURAL RESOURCES: things that exist in or are formed by nature

Natural Resources

Minerals and rocks:

Crushed stone
Zinc
Cement
Sand
Gravel
Coal
Limestone
Marble
Sandstone
Petroleum
Barite
Lead
Lime
Agate

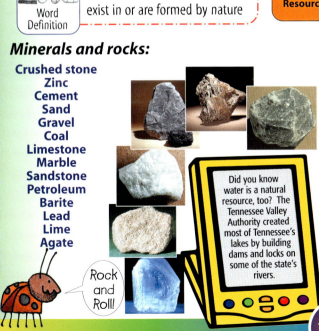

Did you know water is a natural resource, too? The Tennessee Valley Authority created most of Tennessee's lakes by building dams and locks on some of the state's rivers.

Rock and Roll!

Weather

Weather, Or Not?!

Tennessee's temperatures can drop to an average of 28°F (-2°C) in the winter and rise to an average of 92°F (33°C) in the summer.

Weather

Highest temperature: 113°F (45°C), Perryville, August 9, 1930

°F=Degrees Fahrenheit °C=Degrees Celsius

Lowest temperature: -32°F (-35°C), Mountain City, December 30, 1917

Tennessee has hot muggy summers, mild winters, and plenty of rain. Snowfall is light in Middle and West Tennessee, but the mountains of East Tennessee may get heavy snows.

Topography

BACK ON TOP

East, Middle, and West Tennessee
Tennessee's topography can be divided into east, middle, and west. East Tennessee has mountains, ridges, coves, and valleys. Middle Tennessee has high hills and a basin with rich farmland. Nestled between the Tennessee River and the Mississippi River are the rolling hills and flatlands of West Tennessee.

Word Definition
TOPOGRAPHY: the detailed mapping of the features of a small area or district

Topography

Sea Level
100 m / 328 ft
200 m / 656 ft
500 m / 1,640 ft
1,000 m / 3,281 ft
2,000 m / 6,562 ft
5,000 m / 16,404 ft

The Nashville Basin is similar to the Bluegrass Basin of Kentucky. Both regions are famous for raising fine horses.

Mountains and Ranges

King of the Hill

Mountains

Clingmans Dome
Mount Guyot
Mount LeConte
Cliff Top
Mount Buckley
Mount Love

Mountains and Ranges

Ranges

Appalachian Mountains
(oldest mountain chain in North America)
Great Smoky Mountains
Unakas (Blue Ridge Mountains)

Rivers

Down The River

Here are some of Tennessee's major rivers:

- **Mississippi River**
- **Tennessee River**
- **Cumberland River**
- **French Broad River**
- **Clinch River**
- **Nantahala River**
- **Little River**
- **Ocoee River**
- **Wolf River**
- **Buffalo River**
- **Nolichucky River**

Rivers

The Ocoee River is rated one of the top white water recreational rivers in the U.S. The Ocoee was the site of the 1996 Olympic white water canoe and kayak competition.

Grab a paddle!

Major Lakes

Gone Fishin'

Major Lakes

- REELFOOT LAKE
- BARKLEY RESERVOIR
- CHEROKEE LAKE
- NICKAJACK LAKE
- CHICKAMAUGA LAKE
- DALE HOLLOW LAKE
- KENTUCKY LAKE
- NORRIS LAKE
- OLD HICKORY LAKE
- PICKWICK LAKE
- LOST SEA – AMERICA'S LARGEST UNDERGROUND LAKE

> Reelfoot Lake is Tennessee's largest natural lake. Reelfoot Lake in northwestern Tennessee was formed by the New Madrid earthquakes of 1811 and 1812.

Word Definition

RESERVOIR: a body of water stored for public use

Cities & Towns

ARE YOU A CITY MOUSE... OR A COUNTRY MOUSE?

Overall, Henry found it Difficult to Cross Plains but had New Hope Goin to Pleasantville.

Have you heard of these wonderful Tennessee town, city, or crossroad names? Perhaps you can start your own list!

Cities & Towns

MAJOR CITIES:
- Memphis
- Nashville
- Knoxville
- Chattanooga
- Clarksville
- Jackson
- Johnson City
- Murfreesboro
- Kingsport
- Oak Ridge
- Columbia

UNIQUE NAMES:
- Ducktown
- Blanche
- Martha
- Henry
- Eva
- Friendship
- Difficult
- Buffalo Valley
- Crab Orchard
- Overall
- Pleasantville
- New Hope
- Cross Plains
- Lucy
- Goin

Bristol is known as the "Birthplace of Country Music."

Transportation

Major Interstate Highways

I-75, I-40, I-24, I-65, I-23, I-81, I-64, and I-51. Tennessee is served by over 86,000 miles (138,400 kilometers) of highways. I-40 is the main east to west route which links Tennessee's principal cities.

Transportation

Railroads

Tennessee has more than 2,500 miles (4,023 kilometers) of railroad tracks. Memphis is an important railroad junction.

Major Airports

Tennessee has more than 160 airports. Nashville, Memphis, and Knoxville have the three leading airports in the state.

Waterways and Ports

Memphis is Tennessee's main port, on the east bank of the Mississippi River. Memphis is the second largest inland port in the U.S. The Tennessee River and the Cumberland River are navigable and are joined by a canal.

Timeline

1540	Spanish explore Tennessee
1673	British arrive in the Tennessee River Valley
1682	French claim Mississippi River Valley
1714	French establish trading post at French Lick
1750	Dr. Thomas Walker leads explorers through upper East Tennessee and discovers Cumberland Gap
1769	William Bean builds first permanent European settlement on Boone's Creek
1772	Watauga Association adopts one of North America's first written documents of self-government
1775	Transylvania Land Company buys Cherokee land
1780	Settlers sign Cumberland Compact
1789	North Carolina gives Tennessee region to the United States
1815	Andrew Jackson and Tennessee volunteers defeat British at the Battle of New Orleans
1818	Jackson Purchase acquires Chickasaw lands
1838	Cherokees march to Oklahoma on the Trail of Tears
1848	Tennesseans volunteer for Mexican-American War
1861	Civil War begins; Tennessee secedes
1933	Tennessee Valley Authority established
1866	Tennessee is readmitted to Union
1983	Nashville Metropolitan Board of Education settles 28-year dispute over school desegregation
1989	Tennessee celebrates 200th anniversary of the United States presidency by honoring state's three native sons who became president
2003	Tennessee aquarium beaks ground on new saltwater exhibit expansion

Early History

Here come the humans!

Early History

Until recently, scientists believed that the first humans came to North America about 14,000 years ago. These people crossed over a land bridge between Siberia and Alaska and then spread out across the North American continent. New evidence now suggests that people may have first arrived at the Americas 15,000, 20,000 or even 30,000 years ago!

These prehistoric people were ancestors of the mound builders that lived in present-day Tennessee. Around AD 1000, farming began to replace hunting as the way of life for these early Tennesseans.

These early people were nomadic hunters who traveled in small bands. They camped when seasons offered hunting, fishing, and fruit and nut gathering.

Early Indians

Native Americans Once Ruled!

Mound Builders lived along the rivers of Tennessee about one thousand years ago. They built their homes and temples on top of large earth mounds. They built smaller mounds to bury their dead. Presents were placed at the burial sites, probably as gifts to help the dead in the afterlife.

Early Indians

The Mound Builders disappeared and were followed by tribes of Native Americans—Cherokee, Creek, Chickasaw, and Shawnee.

Word Definition

WAMPUM: beads, pierced and strung, used by Indians as money or for ornaments

Exploration

Land Ho!

During the 1540s, Spanish explorers passed through present-day Tennessee looking for gold. British explorers followed about a hundred years later. They were looking for treasures and new lands. French explorers canoed down the Mississippi River in 1682 and claimed the entire Mississippi River Valley for France. The French had come to stay. In 1714, a French trading post was built at French Lick, near present-day Nashville.

In the early 1700s, France, Spain, and Great Britain had claims on Tennessee. By 1754, Spain no longer claimed ownership, leaving the region of Tennessee to France and Great Britain.

Exploration

Pioneers lived in small, isolated settlements. They built forts for protection. In 1772, they formed the Watauga Association and adopted one of North America's first written documents of self-government.

Colonization

Home, Sweet Home

The French and Indian War started in 1754. When the war ended in 1763, France had lost to Great Britain. French lands east of the Mississippi River were now under British control. Tennessee became part of the British colony of North Carolina.

After Britain gained control of the Tennessee region (now part of North Carolina), settlers from Pennsylvania, Virginia, and North Carolina began crossing into the region of Tennessee.

Colonization

Richard Henderson, of North Carolina, was interested in the lands beyond the Appalachian Mountains. He formed the Transylvania Land Company and hired a skilled woodsman and longhunter named Daniel Boone to cut trails into the unexplored regions. Boone cut a trail through the mountains at Cumberland Gap called the Wilderness Trail which became the main route into Tennessee.

Longhunters, like Daniel Boone, would often travel for months, or even years, at a time in the wilderness exploring and hunting.

Key Crops

Nearly one half of Tennessee is farmland. Soybeans and tobacco are the most important crops and grow in East and Middle Tennessee. Cotton grows in West Tennessee.

Livestock produces more than half of the state's agricultural income. Cattle, hogs, and sheep are raised in Middle Tennessee where the grazing land is good for the livestock. The famous Tennessee Walking Horse is also raised in Middle Tennessee near Nashville.

Key Crops

In colonial times, tobacco was called the sot weed and many other ugly names by those who thought smoking and snuff were bad habits!

Legends and Lore

The Day It Rained *Snakes?!*

On January 15, 1877, the weather in Memphis took a strange, slithering twist! Clouds rolled in, and it began to rain. Not a gentle rain, but a torrential, frog-strangler. Folks in the southern part of Memphis got more than rain—they got snakes!

Over a few city blocks, snakes rained down. Not just a few, and not just little ones! Thousands of black snakes, fell from the sky! Several days after the storm, there were still snakes up to 18 inches (46 centimeters) long, slithering around on the ground.

The story got national attention, including a report in *The New York Times*. But so far, no one has come up with a really good explanation. What do *you* think caused this weird, wild weather phenomenon?

Legends and Lore

Revolution

Freedom! Freedom!

Some settlers in the New World felt that England ignored their ideas and concerns. In 1775, the colonies went to war with England. On July 4, 1776, the Declaration of Independence was signed.

Revolution

Tennesseans fought bravely in the Revolutionary War against British and Loyalist troops and their Native American allies. In 1780, Tennessee riflemen fought and defeated British forces at the Battle of Kings Mountain in South Carolina, a major battle and turning point of the war in the South.

Following the Revolutionary War, North Carolina gave up its claim to Tennessee. Tennesseans made plans to form a new state called Franklin. But the new state of Franklin was short-lived as North Carolina reclaimed the Tennessee region.

> In 1789, North Carolina again ceded claims to Tennessee, this time for good. This action paved the way for statehood. Tennessee joined the Union as the 16th state on June 1, 1796.

Slaves and Slavery

Early in Tennessee's history, slaves were brought to serve on plantations. While not all farmers owned slaves, some plantation owners could only run their farms with slave labor.

Slaves could be sold whenever their owners chose to do so. Men, women, and children could be taken from their families—separated at any time! Long days, hard labor, disease, and bad weather made plantation life one of misery.

Slaves and Slavery

Many slaves shared unique talents, such as creating some of the favorite foods we enjoy today from recipes or seeds they brought from Africa. They also fought for freedom in creative ways. Slave women created quilts with secret designs to help those wishing to escape find their way along the famous Underground Railroad.

Word Definition

ABOLITIONIST: person who believed slavery was wrong and should be ended

The Civil War

The Civil War was fought between the American states from 1861 to 1865. The argument was over states' rights to make their own decisions, including whether or not to own slaves. Southern states, with plantations and slaves, were on one side of this conflict. Northern states, who opposed slavery or had no need of it, were on the other side.

The Civil War

Some of the southern states began to secede (leave) the Union. They formed the Confederate States of America. Tennessee was the last southern state to secede and the first to be readmitted after the war ended. Tennessee sent more soldiers into battle than any other state.

After four long years, the Confederacy

Word Definition

RECONSTRUCTION: the recovery and rebuilding period following the Civil War

The Civil War

vs. Brother

surrendered at Appomattox Court House in Virginia. It took years for the country to recover from the devastation of this unfortunate war, in which Americans could find no way to agree, except to fight!

The Civil War was also called the War Between the States. Soldiers often found themselves fighting against former friends and neighbors, even brother against brother. Those who did survive often went home without an arm, leg, or both, since amputation was the "cure" for most battlefield wounds. More Americans were killed during the Civil War than during World Wars I and II together!

The Civil War

In 1865, at the end of the Civil War, the 13th Amendment was ratified! This amendment abolished slavery throughout the United States. Some slaves became sharecroppers, others went north to work in factories.

Famous Documents

Get It In Writing!

1772
Watauga Association Constitution, America's first self-governing document

1775
Transylvania Purchase, treaty took Cherokee lands

Famous Documents

1776
Declaration of Independence

1787
The *Tennessee Gazette,* first Nashville newspaper

1789
U.S. Constitution

1796
First state constitution

1819
Manumission Intelligencer, first antislavery paper in the U.S.

Immigrants

WELCOME TO AMERICA!

People have come to Tennessee from other states and many other countries on almost every continent! As time goes by, Tennessee's population grows more diverse. This means that people of different races and from different cultures and ethnic backgrounds have moved to Tennessee. All Tennesseans benefit from this diverse culture!

In the past, many immigrants came to Tennessee from Britain, Scotland, Ireland, Germany, Wales, and Italy. More recently, Asians, Hispanics, and Pacific Islanders have migrated to Tennessee. The state is proud of its heritage, including Native-Americans and African-Americans.

Only a certain number of immigrants are allowed to move to America each year. Many of these immigrants eventually become U.S. citizens.

Immigrants

Disasters & Catastrophes!

The Big Quake!

During the winter of 1811–1812, violent earthquakes erupt and change the northwestern Tennessee landscape. A crack opens between the Mississippi River and Cypress Bottoms. For three days during the earthquakes, the Mississippi River flows backward and fills the bottoms, creating Reelfoot Lake.

Seek Shelter Immediately!

In March 1952, 67 people die and 282 are injured as ten tornadoes tear through Tennessee. Damages exceed $5.5 million!

No Way Out!

In 1911, near Briceville in Anderson County, an explosion and flash fire destroys Cross Mountain Coal Mine No. 1. Of the 89-member crew, 84 perish in the flames!

In 1902, Tennessee's worst coal mine accident occurs at nearby Fraterville Mine— 184 miners are lost!

A Deadly Disease!

After World War I ends, a catastrophic Spanish flu pandemic (world-wide epidemic) breaks out in Tennessee. More than 7,700 people die!

Legal Stuff

You Must Leave Your Homes!

The Indian Removal Act of 1830 enables the U.S. government to force Cherokee in the East to leave their homes and move west of the Mississippi River. In 1838, about 14,000 Cherokee are brutally marched west. At least a fourth die before they reach Oklahoma!

Man Came From Monkeys?

During July 1925, Dayton becomes the focus of world attention as teacher John Scopes goes on trial for teaching evolution. Well-known attorneys William Jennings Bryan and Clarence Darrow square off in the courtroom. Bryan wins. Scopes is found guilty, but the verdict is set aside because of a legal error.

The summer of 1925 was hot—inside the courtroom and out! Nearby Robinson's Drugstore sells a bunch of cool drinks called Monkey Fizzes to interested spectators.

Road Kill Bill

In 1999, the "Road Kill Bill" passes making it legal to keep and consume wild game, such as deer and bear, killed accidentally by vehicles.

Women & Children

Don't be Late for Class!

In 1837, Tennessee creates a uniform system of public schools.

Help for the Kids!

In 1911, the Tennessee General Assembly passes a child labor law to protect kids who have to go to work!

Women & Children

Finally, the Right to Vote!

In 1919, Tennessee enacts a bill giving women the right to vote. In 1920, Tennessee is the 36th and deciding state to ratify the 19th Amendment giving women across the nation the right to vote!

Equal Rights!

In 1954, U.S. Supreme Court rules that segregation is illegal in public schools. Desegregation begins in Clinton in 1956. Finally, in 1983, the Nashville Metropolitan Board of Education settles the 28-year old courtroom battle over desegregation!

Wars

Fight! Fight! Fight!

Wars that Tennesseans fought in:

- French and Indian War
- Revolutionary War
- War of 1812
- Mexican-American War
- Civil War
- Spanish-American War
- World War I
- World War II
- Korean War
- Vietnam War
- Persian Gulf War
- War on Terror

Music! Music! Music!

Tennessee is a land of music, music, music! East Tennessee has its Appalachian folk songs and bluegrass. Middle Tennessee is the home of country music, and West Tennessee created blues and rock 'n' roll.

Nashville's rise to "Music City, USA" began back in 1925 when an insurance company started a radio station. WSM broadcast a program entitled "Barn Dance" that featured folk music from the Appalachian Mountains. The ballads of folk music blossomed into the songs of "country music" and in 1927, the show's name was changed to "The Grand Ole Opry."

Music! Music! Music!

Memphis, on the other side of the state, has distinctly different musical traditions. Rhythm and blues is a style of music developed by African-Americans. The rhythmic sounds of the blues gave birth to another form of popular American music known as rock 'n' roll!

The Grand Ole Opry is the longest continuously running live radio program in the world! It's been broadcast every week since 1925. *Live from the Grand Ole Opry…!*

Indian Tribes

Cherokee, northern part of East and Middle Tennessee

Creek, southeast Tennessee

Chickasaw, West Tennessee

Shawnee, Middle Tennessee

Almost half of the Cherokee in Tennessee were wiped out by European diseases to which they had no immunity. It is believed these diseases, including smallpox, were intentionally introduced by the settlers through blankets and other trade goods in 1738 in order to wipe out the Cherokee tribe.

Indian Tribes

Creek, Cherokee, and Chickasaw were forced from their homelands to make way for settlers. The Transylvania Purchase and other treaties took lands from the Native American tribes.

The Indians of Tennessee could not have known that the coming of the white man would mean an end to the way of life they had known for hundreds of years.

Explorers and Settlers

Here, There, Everywhere!

Hernando de Soto—Spanish explorer; crossed Tennessee in 1540 with missionaries and conquistadors searching for gold

Father Jacques Marquette of France and **Louis Jolliet of Canada**—explored Mississippi River in 1670s

René-Robert Cavelier, Sieur de La Salle—French explorer; claimed entire Mississippi River Valley for France in 1682

Charles Charleville—French trader; established trading post at French Lick (present-day Nashville) in 1714

Explorers and Settlers

Dr. Thomas Walker—Virginia colonist and explorer; explored and named Cumberland Gap in 1750; discovered and named the Cumberland River

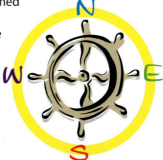

State Founders

Founding Fathers

William Bean—built cabin on Boone's Creek; started first permanent European settlement in Tennessee

Thomas "Big Foot" Spencer—longhunter; pioneer; first settler to clear land and plant corn in Middle Tennessee

David Crockett—born in Limestown; frontiersman; soldier; politician; military scout; killed in 1836 at the Alamo in Texas

Timothy Demonbreun—French-Canadian fur trader; merchant; "Nashville's First Citizen"

Founding Mother

***Nanye'hi* (Nancy Ward), Beloved Woman**—Cherokee; fought bravely alongside her husband at the Battle of Taliwa against Creek; when her husband was killed, *Nanye'hi* rallied the Cherokee warriors and led them to victory; Cherokee named her *Aqiqa-u-e,* or Beloved Woman, a title of honor given only to women of great influence; served as Cherokee leader for more than 50 years

Famous African-Americans

Dr. Emma Rochelle Wheeler—established Walden Hospital for African-Americans in Chattanooga; founded a nursing school; worked to improve medical treatment for African-Americans

W.C. Handy—blues musician and composer; known as the Father of the Blues; prestigious honor for blues artist, the W.C. Handy Award is named in his honor; best-known song is "St. Louis Blues"; also wrote "Memphis Blues"; wrote blues songs on Beale Street in Memphis

Bessie Smith—powerful singer with a rich, deep voice; known as "Empress of the Blues"; successfully blended African and Western music to create a distinctive "blues-jazz" sound

Famous African-Americans

Dr. Dorothy Brown—surgeon, educator, legislator; first African-American woman to practice surgery in the South; first African-American woman elected to General Assembly

---

Dr. Martin Luther King, Jr., civil-rights leader, was assassinated on April 4, 1968, in Memphis. He was in the city for a sanitation workers' strike to improve working conditions. The National Civil Rights Museum is located at the Lorraine Motel where Dr. King was killed.

Ghost

DID SOMEONE SAY BOO!?

One of Tennessee's most famous ghost stories is the tale (or tales) of the Bell Witch. "Kate" tormented the family of John and Lucy Bell, a wealthy couple who lived on a farm in Adams.

"Kate" slapped, pinched, and pulled the hair of family members; took covers off beds while people were sleeping; recited prayers; imitated the voices of local people; threw furniture; sang to visitors; and quoted scriptures from the Bible.

Andrew Jackson visited the Bell family to confront the famous ghost. "Kate" told the future president, "All right, General, I am on hand, ready for business!" And apparently, she was!

DO YOU BELIEVE IN GHOSTS?

Sports Stuff

John Ward—"Voice of the Vols"; announcer for University of Tennessee football games; *"Touchdown, Big Orange!"* and *"Give him six!"*

Melanie Smith—equestrian, jumper; first woman to win prestigious American Gold Cup

Peyton Manning—popular University of Tennessee star quarterback; among his many awards is the Sullivan Award for the number-one amateur athlete in the U.S.

Tracy Caulkins—Olympic gold-medal swimmer; won 48 national titles; set 61 national and five world records

Wilma Rudolph—Olympic gold-medal track and field athlete; overcame polio as a child; set world record for women's 100-meter dash in 1961

Robert Reese Neyland, Jr.—head football coach and athletic director at the University of Tennessee; soldier; professor; brigadier general in U.S. Army

Ted Rhodes—professional golfer; in 1961, broke through racial barriers prohibiting African-Americans from playing in the Professional Golf Association

Pat Head Summitt—successful coach of National Champion Lady Vols; elected to Basketball Hall of Fame in 2000

Very Important People

Casey Jones—railroad engineer; killed in a famous train wreck; his home in Jackson is now a museum

Wallace Saunders—an African-American from Tennessee rode with Jones and wrote "The Ballad of Casey Jones"—one of America's most popular folk ballads

Nat Love—cowboy; most famous African-American cowboy of the American West; earned nickname "Deadwood Dick" for shooting, roping, and riding skills

Danny Thomas—entertainer; humanitarian; founder of St. Jude Children's Hospital in Memphis

Dr. Rhea Seddon—one of first six women in space; traveled to space for seven days aboard the space shuttle *Discovery*

Edward E. Barnard—astronomer; discovered Jupiter's fifth moon; found 16 comets; pioneer of celestial photography

Sue Shelton White—attorney, writer, suffragist, political activist, member of Tennessee Equal Suffrage Association and National Woman's Party; edited *Suffragist* newspaper; lobbied for ratification of 19th Amendment giving women the right to vote throughout the U.S.

Very Important People

Authors

- **James Agee**—author; won a Pulitzer Prize for his novel, *A Death in the Family;* wrote screenplays including *The African Queen*

- **Mary Noailles Murfree**—author; wrote under pen name of Charles E. Craddock; wrote *The Frontiersman, In the Tennessee Mountains,* and *In the Clouds*

- **Alex Haley**—author; won Pulitzer Prize for *Roots;* collaborated on *The Autobiography of Malcolm X*

- **Thomas Lanier Williams**—famous playwright; chose pen name of Tennessee Williams for fond memories of childhood in Nashville

- **Elizabeth Gilmer**—journalist and author; wrote under pen name Dorothy Dix; wrote *How To Win and Hold a Husband*

- **Adolph S. Ochs**—publisher; owner and publisher of *Chattanooga Times* and *The New York Times;* coined the phrase, "All the news that's fit to print."

- **Ida B. Wells Barnett**—African-American educator, journalist, social reformer; fought for equal rights and to improve conditions for African-Americans

Alex Haley's boyhood home in Henning is the first state-owned historic site honoring an African-American in Tennessee.

Artists

Kate Augusta Carl—painter, educator; best-known for portrait of last Empress Dowager of China

William Edmondson—sculptor; first African-American artist to have a one-man show at the Museum of Modern Art in New York

Emma Bell Miles—painter, author, teacher; eloquently wrote about life in the mountains of Tennessee

Clark Byers—painted most of the more than 800 barns in 19 states that told travelers to "See Rock City"

Artists

The Appalachian Mountains are famous for celebrated crafts and craftspeople. Handmade quilts, pottery, baskets, furniture, musical instruments, fabrics, and toys such as dolls and gee-haw-whimmy-diddles were everyday necessities for self-reliant pioneers. The rich frontier heritage continues today as many traditional arts and crafts have been handed down through the generations. Today, these artforms are also studied at various schools throughout the region.

Performing Artists

Elvis Presley—"The King"; legendary rock 'n' roll singer; many popular songs include "Love Me Tender" and "Are You Lonesome Tonight"; starred in many hit movies

Rock 'n' roll and blues greats—Jerry Lee Lewis, Carl Perkins, B.B. King, Muddy Waters, Howlin' Wolf

Dolly Parton—country music singer and songwriter; starred in movies including *Nine to Five* and *Steel Magnolias*; creator of Dollywood Theme Park in Pigeon Forge

Dinah Shore—singer, actress; always ended her performance with a big kiss thrown to her audience

Grace Moore—opera singer; known as "the Tennessee Nightingale"; sang in New York on Broadway and at the Metropolitan Opera

Performing Artists

Quentin Tarantino—director; films include *Reservoir Dogs* and *Pulp Fiction*

Morgan Freeman—actor; movies include *Driving Miss Daisy, Unforgiven,* and *Robin Hood: Prince of Thieves*

Tennessee Ernie Ford—singer; songs include "Sixteen Tons"; always ended TV show with "Bless your little ol' pea-picking hearts"

Tina Turner—singer, actress; began her singing career in the choir of Spring Hill Baptist Church

Dixie Carter, Annie Potts—actresses; two of TV's *Designing Women*

Performing Artists

A Few of the Many Country Music Legends: Kitty Wells • Webb Pierce • Lefty Frizzell • Bill Monroe • Del Reeves • Faron Young • Minnie Pearl • Sonny James • Little Jimmy Dickens • Dottie West • Charlie Pride • Homer & Jethro • Roy Acuff • Eddy Arnold • Loretta Lynn • Tammy Wynette • Chet Atkins • Johnny Cash • June Carter Cash • Carter Family • George Jones • Porter Wagoner • Hank Williams (Sr. and Jr.) • Patsy Cline

Kathy Bates—Oscar-winning actress; films include *Misery*, *Fried Green Tomatoes*, and *Annie*

Amy Grant—singer; successfully records contemporary Christian and pop songs

Lester Flatt—bluegrass music legend; half of Flatt & Scruggs with Earl Scruggs

Aretha Franklin—singer; known for soulful songs such as "R-E-S-P-E-C-T," "Natural Woman," "Chain of Fools," and "Think"

Jim Varney—actor; films include *Ernest Goes to Camp* and *Ernest Saves Christmas*

The Gaithers—along with their homecoming friends, Bill and Gloria Gaither sing the sweet sounds of southern gospel

Oprah Winfrey—actress; talk-show hostess; news reporter; first Miss Black Tennessee

Cybill Shepherd—actress; TV shows include *Moonlighting*, first movie was *The Last Picture Show*

Polly Bergen—Emmy-winning actress; films include *The Helen Morgan Story*

Political Leaders

John Sevier—governor of the "lost" state of Franklin; first governor of Tennessee, served for six terms; U.S. Congressman

Ann Lee Worley—first woman in the nation to be elected state senator

Estes Kefauver—U.S. senator; vice-presidential candidate; remembered for wearing coonskin cap

Al Gore—U.S. senator; U.S. congressman; vice president; presidential candidate

Tipper Gore—wife of Al Gore; wrote best-selling book *Raising PG Kids in an X-Rated Society* which addressed the impact of entertainment industry on kids

Political Leaders

Julian Bond—civil rights leader, politician; first African-American to be nominated for office of vice president of the U.S.

Camille McGee Kelley—first woman judge in the South; second woman judge in the nation

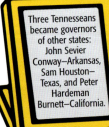

Three Tennesseans became governors of other states: John Sevier Conway–Arkansas, Sam Houston–Texas, and Peter Hardeman Burnett–California.

Sampson W. Keeble—first African-American elected to General Assembly

Julia Doak—first woman to hold the office of state superintendent of education in the nation

Good Guys, Patriots, and Heroes

Sergeant Alvin York—soldier; humanitarian; World War I hero; used effective combat tactics; received Medal of Honor

Sequoyah—Cherokee silversmith; created written language for Cherokee Nation; only man ever known to develop an alphabet on his own; Sequoyah Birthplace Museum in Vonore dedicated to history and culture of Native Americans

Cornelia Fort—aviator; first woman pilot to die serving her country; killed in mid-air collision during World War II

John Ross—chief of United Cherokee Nation; president of the National Council of Cherokees; resisted removal, but finally led nation to Oklahoma

Andrew Jackson—7th U.S. president; hero of Battle of New Orleans; helped Tennessee become a state; nickname was "Old Hickory"

James Polk—11th U.S. president; during his presidency, much of the West became part of the U.S.

Andrew Johnson—17th U.S. president; elected to offices at local, state, and federal levels; one of his last official acts was to pardon all Southerners who fought in the Civil War

Samuel Powhatan Carter of Elizabethton is the only American to have been both an admiral in the Navy and a general in the Army.

Churches and Schools

Keeping the Faith

- **Saint Paul's Episcopal Church**, Franklin
- **Greeneville Cumberland Presbyterian Church**
- **Christ Church, Episcopal**, Rugby
- **Sinking Creek Baptist Church**, between Elizabethton and Johnson City
- **New Salem Missionary Church**, Carthage
- **Saint Peter's Catholic Church**, Memphis

SCHOOLS

- **University of Tennessee** with campuses in Memphis, Knoxville, Martin, Tullahoma, and Chattanooga
- **Vanderbilt University**, Nashville—includes George Peabody College for Teachers
- **Tusculum College**, Greeneville
- **Fisk University**, Nashville
- **Tennessee State University**, Nashville
- **Meharry Medical College**, Nashville
- **Carson-Newman College**, Jefferson City
- **University of the South**, Sewanee
- **Lincoln Memorial University**, Harrogate
- **Austin Peay State University**, Clarksville
- **University of Memphis**
- **Middle Tennessee State University**, Murfreesboro

Historic Sites and Parks

HISTORIC SITES

Cades Cove, Townsend, Smokies
Chucalissa Prehistoric Indian Village, Memphis
Sergeant Alvin C. York Historic Area, Jamestown
Historic Blackburn Farmstead and Pioneer Museum, Hohenwald
Mound Bottom, Kingston Springs
Andrew Johnson National Historic Site, Greeneville
Humphrey's County Museum and Civil War Fort, Waverly
Cumberland Gap National Historical Park
Scopes Trial Museum and Rhea County Courthouse, Dayton
Volunteer State Veterans Hall of Honor, Knoxville
Beale Street Historic District, Memphis
The Felsenthal Lincoln Collection, Brownsville
Dunlap Coke Ovens Historic Site and Museum of Mining Artifacts

PARKS

Great Smoky Mountains National Park—most visited national park in the nation; gets its name from the smoke-like bluish haze that usually covers the mountains
Cordell Hull Birthplace State Park, Byrdstown
Reelfoot Lake State Park, Tiptonville
Sycamore Shoals State Park
Pinson Mounds State Archaeological Park, Jackson
Davy Crockett Birthplace State Park, Limestone
Cherokee National Forest
Cedars of Lebanon State Park, east of Nashville
Land between the Lakes, Dover

Home, Sweet Home!

Graceland, Memphis—home of Elvis Presley; second most visited house in the U.S. (the White House is Number One)

Jacob Burkle Estate, Memphis—Burkle was a "conductor" on the Underground Railroad; his Memphis home was a "station" for slaves making their escape to freedom in the North

The Hermitage, Nashville—home of President Andrew and Rachel Jackson; Gibson Guitar Company used timber from trees downed during 1998 tornado to create Hermitage Guitars

Carter Mansion, Elizabethton—home of John and Landon Carter; one of oldest and most influential houses in Tennessee

Belle Meade Plantation, Nashville—during the Civil War, Elizabeth McGavock Harding assumed duties of running plantation in the absence of her husband General William Giles Harding; known as the Queen of Tennessee Plantations

Rattle and Snap Plantation, Mt. Pleasant—built by George W. Polk; land won during a game of chance called "Rattle and Snap"

James K. Polk Ancestral Home, Columbia—home built in 1816 where James K. Polk began his legal and political career

Battles and Forts

BATTLE SITES AND FORTS

- **Chickamauga/Chattanooga National Military Park**, Chattanooga
- **Shiloh National Military Park and Cemetery**
- **Stones River National Battlefield and Cemetery**, Murfreesboro
- **Spring Hill Battlefield**
- **Fort Donelson National Battlefield and Cemetery**, Dover
- **Fort Defiance**, Clarksville
- **Bledsoe's Fort Historic Park**, Castalian Springs
- **Fort Loudoun State Historic Park**, Vonore
- **Fort Nashborough**, Nashville
- **Fort Campbell Military Reservation/Don F. Pratt Museum**, Clarkesville

MAJOR CIVIL WAR BATTLES

More Civil War battles were fought in the state of Tennessee than in all the states other than Virginia.

- **Battle of Fort Donelson**
- **Battle of Shiloh**
- **Battle of Stones River**
- **Battle of Chattanooga**
- **Battle of Franklin**
- **Battle of Nashville**

Battles and Forts

Libraries

Check out the following special Tennessee libraries! (Do you have a library card? Have you worn it out yet?!)

Memphis Public Library
Nashville Public Library
Knoxville Public Library
Chattanooga Public Library
Thomas Hughes Free Public Library, Rugby
State Library and Archives, Nashville
Vanderbilt University Library, Nashville
Vanderbilt Medical School Library
University of Tennessee Libraries at Chattanooga, Knoxville, Martin, Memphis, and Tullahoma
Le Moyne-Owen College Library, Memphis
Lincoln Memorial University Library, Harrogate
Fisk University Library, Nashville

Libraries

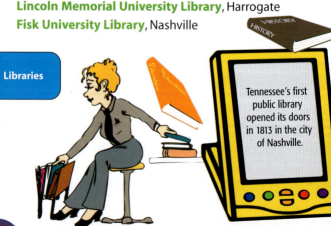

Tennessee's first public library opened its doors in 1813 in the city of Nashville.

Zoos and Attractions

Knoxville Zoo, Memphis Zoo, Nashville Zoo, Chattanooga Zoo, Abilene Zoo
Tennessee Aquarium, Chattanooga
Gibson Guitar Plant, Memphis
Christus Gardens, Gatlinburg
Chattanooga Choo Choo
Ducks Unlimited International Headquarters, Memphis
Laurel-Snow Pocket Wilderness and Buzzard Point, Dayton
Memphis Pink Palace Museum and Sharpe Planetarium
Tennessee National Wildlife Refuge, Paris
Bell Witch Cave, Adams
Lookout Mountain Incline Railway, Chattanooga
American Museum of Science and Energy, Oak Ridge
Dollywood, Pigeon Forge
Dunbar Cave State Natural Area, Clarksville
General Jackson Showboat, Nashville
Cheatham Wildlife Management Area, Ashland City
Ruby Falls, Chattanooga
Bristol Motor Speedway
Benton-Houston Ferry, Big Sandy
Big Cypress Tree State Natural Area, Greenfield
Memphis Queen Line Riverboats
Burgess Falls State Natural Area, Cookeville
Ocoee Whitewater Center, Cherokee National Forest

Zoos and Attractions

Museums

Country Music Hall of Fame and Museum, Nashville
Tennessee State Museum, Nashville
National Civil Rights Museum, Memphis
National Bird Dog Museum, Field Trial Hall of Fame and Wildlife Heritage Center, Grand Junction
National Ornamental Metal Museum, Memphis
Carbo's Smoky Mountain Police Museum, Pigeon Forge
Museum of Appalachia, Norris
Elvis Museum, Pigeon Forge
Medal of Honor Museum of Military History, Chattanooga
Tennessee River Folklife Interpretive Center, Camden
The Children's Museum of Memphis
Women's Basketball Hall of Fame, Knoxville
Memphis Music Hall of Fame
Museum of Magic and History, Dyersburg
Tennessee Walking Horse Museum, Shelbyville
Cumberland Science Museum, Nashville
Tennessee Civil War Museum, Chattanooga
Little River Railroad and Lumber Company Museum, Townsend
Southern Gospel Music Hall of Fame and Museum, Pigeon Forge
Children's Museum of Oak Ridge
Ducktown Basin Museum
Chattanooga African Museum
Trenton Teapot Museum
Tennessee Agricultural Museum, Nashville

Monuments and Memorials

Lest We Forget

First monument to honor an unknown soldier of the Confederacy, Union City

Sequoyah Birthplace Museum, Vonore

Beech Grove Confederate Cemetery and Park

Meriwether Lewis Park, Grave and Monument, Hohenwald

W.C. Handy House Museum, Memphis

Mexican War Monument, Lawrenceburg

Buford Pusser Home and Museum, Adamsville

Standing Stone Monument, Monterey

Sam Houston Schoolhouse, Maryville

Nancy Ward Gravesite, Benton

Patsy Cline Memorial, Camden

The Sleepy John Estes House, Brownsville

Birthplace of Tennessee Ernie Ford, Bristol

Bleak House, Confederate Memorial Hall, Knoxville

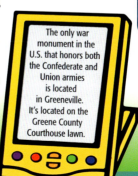

The only war monument in the U.S. that honors both the Confederate and Union armies is located in Greeneville. It's located on the Greene County Courthouse lawn.

Monuments and Memorials

Performing Arts

Nashville Children's Theatre
Blues City Cultural Center, Memphis
Acuff Theatre at Opryland USA, Nashville
Tennessee Valley Theatre, Spring City
Tennessee Performing Arts Center, Nashville
Germantown Performing Arts Centre, Memphis
Grand Ole Opry and Museum, Nashville
Trinity Music City, USA, Hendersonville
Casey Jones Outdoor Music Theater, Jackson
Center for Southern Folklore, Beale Street, Memphis
Orpheum Theater, Memphis
"The Wataugans" Outdoor Drama, Elizabethton
Gem Theater, Etowah
Beechwood Music Center, Kingsport
Oak Ridge Community Playhouse
Chattanooga Theatre Centre
Ernest Tubb Midnight Jamboree, Nashville
Ryman Auditorium, Nashville
Cumberland County Playhouse, Crossville
Tennessee Repertory Theater, Nashville
The Laster's Bluegrass Opry, Gibson
The American Negro Playwright Theatre, Nashville
Opera Memphis
Nashville Chamber Orchestra

Performing Arts

To be, or not to be involved in the arts—that is the question. What is your answer?

Arts and Crafts

Tellico Arts Center, Tellico Plains
Cherokee Chieftain, Cleveland
Freestone Pottery, Whitleyville
Sarratt Gallery at Vanderbilt University, Nashville
Tullahoma Fine Arts Center/Regional Museum of Art
Wildwoods Folk School, Red Boiling Springs
Coker Creek Crafts Gallery
Arrowmont School of Arts & Crafts, Gatlinburg
Nutbush/Tina Turner Heritage Resource Center
Ewing Gallery of Art and Architecture, Knoxville
Knoxville Museum of Art
Center for Excellence for the Creative Arts, Clarksville
Ashwood Pottery, Columbia
Amish Country Galleries, Ethridge
Appalachian Arts Craft Shop, Norris
Farmhouse Gallery and Gardens, Unicoi
The Johnson City Area Arts Council and Fine Arts Gallery
The Parthenon, Nashville
Hunter Museum of American Art, Chattanooga
Cleveland Creative Arts Guild
Deerfoot Quilts, Cosby
The Arts Center of Cannon County, Woodbury
West Tennessee Regional s Art Center, Humboldt

The largest group of independent artists and craftsmen in the U.S. is the Great Smoky Arts and Crafts Community near Gatlinburg.

Roads, Bridges, and More!

Roads,

Dolly Parton Parkway, Great Smoky Mountains National Park

Cherohala Skyway, Cherokee National Forest

Interstate 40, Music Highway, between Memphis and Nashville

Ocoee Scenic Byway, Cherokee National Forest

Natchez Trace Parkway

Bridges,

Tennessee has 36 natural bridges!

Natchez Trace Parkway Bridge—largest segmented, arched bridge in the U.S.

Doe River Covered Bridge, Elizabethton—thought to be oldest covered bridge in Tennessee still in use

and More!
TRAILS

Overmountain Victory National Historic Trail, Sycamore Shoals

State Historic Area, Elizabethton

Path of the Longhunter, Gallatin

Trail of Tears National Historic Trail

Cumberland River Bicentennial Trail, Ashland City

Appalachian Trail

Caves and Caverns

TENNESSEE HAS MORE THAN 3,800 DOCUMENTED CAVES!

Blue Spring Cave—longest cave in the state

Cumberland Caverns, McMinnville—has largest cave room in eastern America; 3/4 ton (680 kilograms) crystal chandelier in the Volcano Room

Cudjo's Cave, Cumberland Gap National Park—has one of largest stalagmites in the world, 35 feet (11 meters) around and 65 feet (20 meters) high, estimated to be 85 million years old

Bristol Caverns

Southport Saltpeter Cave, Columbia

Forbidden Caverns, Sevierville

Tuckaleechee Caverns, Townsend

Question:
- Which is the stalagmite?
- Which is the stalactite?

ANSWER: Stalactites are long, tapering formations hanging from the roof of a cavern, produced by continuous watery deposits containing certain minerals. The mineral-rich water dripping from stalactites often forms conical stalagmites on the floor below.

Caves and Caverns

Word Definition — SPELUNKER: a person who goes exploring caves for fun

Animals

TENNESSEE'S ANIMALS INCLUDE:

Opossum
Red fox
Gray fox
Bobcat
Muskrat
Bat
Wild boar
Raccoon (state wild animal)
White-tailed deer
Woodchuck
Black bear

Can you guess which animal a spelunker might meet face to face?
A bat is that!

Wildlife Watch

Take a Walk on the Wild Side!

Some endangered Tennessee animals are:

Red-cockaded woodpecker

Carolina northern flying squirrel

Nashville crayfish

Appalachian monkeyface pearly mussel

American peregrine falcon

Oyster mussel

Anthony's riversnail

Pallid sturgeon

Least tern

Indiana bat

Red wolf

Amber darter

Gray bat

Spruce-fir moss spider

Ring pink mussel

Appalachian elktoe

Red wolves have recently been "reintroduced" into their former habitats in the Great Smoky Mountains National Park! That's progress! *Way to go, Tennessee!*

Wildlife Watch

Birds

You may spy these birds in Tennessee:

Bobwhite quail (state game bird)
Mourning dove
Sparrow
Duck
Killdeer
Red-tailed hawk
Woodpecker
Owl
Crow
Carolina chickadee
Wren
Robin
Eastern bluebird
Mockingbird (state bird)
Cardinal
Goldfinch
Hummingbird
Blackbird

A hummingbird's wings beat 75 times a second—so fast that you only see a blur! The birds make short squeaky sounds but do not sing.

Insects

Don't let these Tennessee bugs bug you!

- Firefly (state insect)
- Dragonfly
- Damselfly
- Katydid
- Cricket
- Giant water bug
- Cicada
- Spittlebug
- Whirligig beetle
- Weevil
- Moth
- Mosquito
- Yellow jacket
- Zebra swallowtail (state butterfly)

Honeybee (state agricultural insect)

Praying mantis

Ants

Butterfly

Ladybug beetle (state insect, too)

Grasshopper

Whirligig beetles have two pairs of eyes—one pair looks above the water, the other under it!

Insects

Do we know any of these bugs?

Maybe... Hey, that ladybug is cute!

81

Fish

SWIMMING IN TENNESSEE'S WATERS:

- Smallmouth bass
- Largemouth bass
- Bluegill
- Crappie
- Striper
- Channel catfish
- White bass
- Yellow bass
- Walleye
- Paddlefish
- Muskie
- Trout

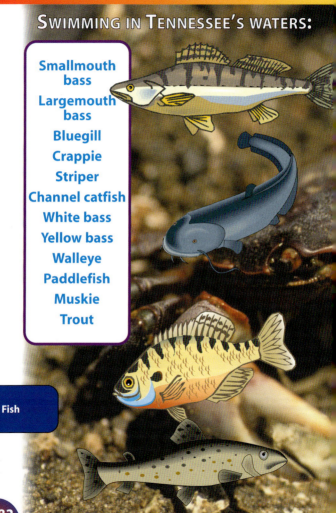

Pond Critters

IN TENNESSEE'S PONDS, YOU MAY FIND:

- Hydra
- Mussel
- Crayfish
- Fishing spider
- Freshwater eel
- Minnow
- Box turtle (state reptile)
- Painted turtle
- Mud puppy
- Eastern newt
- Frog
- Toad

In spring, male bullfrogs compete with each other by wrestling. The winning frog pushes the losing frog onto its back. The prize = female frogs!

Pond Critters

SSSSSSnakes!

NONPOISONOUS SNAKES INCLUDE
- Water snake
- Black rat snake
- Garter snake
- King snake
- Pine snake

POISONOUS SNAKES
- Copperhead
- Cottonmouth
- Timber rattlesnake

SSSSO THE SSSSTORY GOESSSS...

On a hot summer day in 1869, a little girl in Murfreesboro stopped to get a refreshing drink of spring water. Soon after, she began having trouble with her stomach. The problems continued for a long time and no one could figure out why.

Five years later she again sought help. A doctor finally discovered the cause. He reached into the girl's mouth and pulled out a slinky, slithering brown snake—all 23 inches (8 centimeters).

SSSSSSnakes!

Cottonmouth snakes can grow to be more than 6 feet (2 meters) long. Cottonmouths swim with their heads well above the water.

Trees

TREEMENDOUS!

THESE TREES TOWER OVER TENNESSEE:

- **TULIP POPLAR** (state tree)
- **SHORTLEAF PINE**
- **CHESTNUT**
- **BLACK OAK**
- **RED OAK**
- **HICKORY**
- **ASH**
- **GUM MAPLE**
- **SYCAMORE**
- **CYPRESS**
- **COTTONWOOD**
- **BLACK WALNUT**

Wildflowers

Are you crazy about these Tennessee flowers?

- Violet
- Mountain laurel
- Passion flower (state wildflower)
- Goldenrod
- Indian paintbrush
- Cattail
- Black-eyed susan
- Buttercup
- Rhododendron
- Butter-and-eggs
- Creeping phlox
- Oswego tea
- Daisy
- Dutchman's-breeches
- Azaleas
- Queen Anne's lace

Wildflowers

Do you ever think you would eat Butter-and-eggs for a sore throat? Early settlers used this beautiful yellow and orange flower to make a medicine that soothed a scratchy throat!

Flower Power!

Cream of the Crops

Agricultural products from Tennessee:

Cotton

Tobacco

Soybeans

Tennessee Walking Horses

Cattle

Corn

Chickens

Tomatoes

Cabbages

Eggs

Dairy products

Wheat

Cream of the Crops

Hay

Strawberries

Apples

Peaches

First/Biggest/Smallest/Etc

Moon Pies® were **first made** in 1917 in Chattanooga. The Chattanooga Bakery Company bakes about 300,000 Moon Pies a day.

Little Debbie® Snack Cakes were **first baked** in 1960 by McKee Foods in Collegedale. Little Debbies were named after little Debbie, a granddaughter of the founder.

Big Bill, the **world's largest pig**, was raised in Tennessee. Big Bill was almost 9 feet (3 meters) long and weighed 2,552 pounds (1,158 kilograms)!

Citizens Savings Bank and Trust Company, the nation's **oldest** African-American financial firm, is located in Nashville.

The **Tennessee Aquarium** in Chattanooga is the **world's largest freshwater aquarium**. There are 7,000 fish, birds, reptiles, amphibians, and mammals.

Ober Gatlinburg Ski Resort has the world's **largest** artificial skiing surface that permits skiing in any type of weather!

Clarence Saunders of Memphis created the world's **first supermarket** and named it **Piggly Wiggly**!

The Seeing Eye started in Nashville in 1928. It's the **first** U.S. organization to train guide dogs for the blind. Morris Frank was the first American to have a Seeing Eye dog, and Buddy, a German shepherd, was that helpful dog!

Festivals and Events

celebrate!

Standing Stone Native American Celebration, Monterey

Reelfoot Eagle Watch Tours, Tiptonville

Great River Carnival, Memphis

International Country Music Fan Fair, Nashville

National Storytelling Festival, Jonesborough

Mule Day, Columbia

Dumas Walker (King of Marbles) Rolley Hole World Championship, Celina

Iris Festival, Greeneville

Covered Bridge Celebration, Elizabethton

Dulcimer and Harp Festival, Crosby

Tennessee State Fair, Nashville

Upper Cumberland Quilt Festival, Algood

Old Time Bluegrass and Fiddler's Championship, Holladay

Tennessee River Folklife and Music Festival, Eva

Smoky Mountains Winterfest, Gatlinburg, Pigeon Forge, Sevierville

Old-Time Fiddlers' Jamboree and Crafts Festival, Smithville

Christmas at Graceland, Memphis

Brownsville Blues Festival

Chester County Annual Barbecue Festival, Henderson

Festivals and Events

Holidays

Calendar

Martin Luther King, Jr. Day, *3rd Monday in January*	Groundhog Day, *February 2*	Presidents' Day, *3rd Monday in February*
Memorial Day, *last Monday in May*	Independence Day, *July 4*	Labor Day, *1st Monday in September*
Columbus Day, *2nd Monday in October*	Veterans Day, *November 11*	Thanksgiving, *4th Thursday in November*

Tennessee celebrates its admission to the U.S. on June 1st.

Christmas and Chanukah are very special celebrations in Tennessee.

Famous Food

Tennessee is famous for...

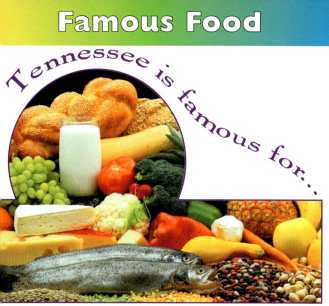

the following foods!

- Fried catfish
- Hushpuppies
- Fried okra
- Cornbread
- Barbecue
- Country ham
- Biscuits
- Sweet tea

- Turnip greens
- Black-eyed peas
- Southern fried chicken
- Green beans
- Corn on the cob
- Pecan pie
- Ramp (onion-like plant)
- Poke salad

Yum, yum. This is great!

Let's dig in!

Famous Food

Business & Trade

Tennessee Works!

Tennessee has a diverse economy with several major industries including the making of chemical products such as paints, medicines, and soaps. Some residents work with food processing in meat-packing plants or canning factories. Many Tennesseans work in the automobile manufacturing industry.

Mining is also an important industry. Tennessee leads the nation in the production of zinc which is used to make pennies, toys, and batteries.

Most Tennesseans hold service-related jobs such as doctor, lawyer, teacher, politician, banker, and salesclerk.

Only about five percent of Tennesseans have jobs in agriculture. But farmland covers about half of Tennessee, so these farmers farm lots of land, grow lots of food, and raise lots of livestock!

> In 1933, the U.S. government created the Tennessee Valley Authority to help control floods, improve navigation, produce electricity, reforest lands, and encourage agricultural and industrial development. This federal act greatly improved the everyday life of Tennessee residents and created lots of jobs!

Tennessee Books & Websites

My First Book About Tennessee by Carole Marsh
America the Beautiful: Tennessee by Sylvia McNair
Kids Learn America by Patricia Gordon and Reed C. Snow
Let's Discover the States: Tennessee by the Aylesworths
The Tennessee Experience Series by Carole Marsh
Hello U.S.A.: Tennessee by Karen Sirvaitis

COOL TENNESSEE WEBSITES

http://www.state.tn.us

http://www.tennesseeexperience.com

http://www.50states.com

http://www.netstate.com

Glossary

Tennessee Glossary

Glossary Words

cavern: large cave

commemorate: to honor

constitution: document outlining the role of a government

desegregation: to stop the practice of keeping people of different races separate

economy: distribution and interplay of wealth and materials within a system

emancipate: to set free

endangered: in danger of becoming extinct or no longer living

evolution: theory that man developed from earlier forms

immigrant: person who comes to a new country to live

prehistoric: time before history was written

reconstruct: to rebuild as before

removal: the act of being taken away

secede: voluntarily give up being a part of an organized group

volunteer: to do something without being forced

Spelling List

Tennessee Spelling Bee

Here are some special Tennessee-related words to learn! To take the Spelling Bee, have someone call out the words and you spell them aloud or write them on a piece of paper.

SPELLING WORDS

- agriculture
- Appalachia
- Cherokee
- Chickasaw
- Choctaw
- Civil War
- Confederacy
- Creek
- East Tennessee
- firefly
- iris
- ladybug
- Middle Tennessee
- mountains
- music
- Nashville
- raccoon
- Shawnee
- Union
- West Tennessee

About the Author

ABOUT THE AUTHOR...

CAROLE MARSH has been writing about Tennessee for more than 20 years. She is the author of the popular Tennessee State Stuff Series for young readers and creator along with her son, Michael Marsh, of Tennessee Facts and Factivities, a CD-ROM widely used in Tennessee schools. The author of more than 100 Tennessee books and other supplementary educational materials on the state, Marsh is currently working on a new collection of Tennessee materials for young people. Marsh correlates her Tennessee materials to the Tennessee learning standards. Many of her books and other materials have been inspired by or requested by Tennessee teachers and librarians.

EDITORIAL ASSISTANT:
Billie Walburn

GRAPHIC DESIGNERS:
Lisa Stanley • Al Fortunatti